Project Future Success

Setting Goals And Working Toward Success

By Simon Wright

Table of Contents

Introduction

This book contains proven steps and strategies on how to set goals, make plans, and improve your way of life in order to achieve success. In this book, you will find a step-by-step guide on exactly how to do this. Furthermore, you will learn how to improve your knowledge, skills, and experience as well as to adjust your mindset to match your plans. You will also learn how to manage your energy levels and conquer your fears, so your journey towards goal fulfillment will be less stressful. Not only that, you will also learn how to create schedules, set priorities, and practice self-discipline to guarantee your success.

Let this book change not just how you view your life, but also how you live it! Get started on your goals now and live your life to the fullest.

Chapter 1 - Set Goals

You have already set goals and probably achieved many of them in the past. A goal stems out from a desire. The more you desire something, the more likely you are to achieve that goal.

However, desire alone cannot provide you with the fuel you need to pursue your goals. It is easy to desire something, but it is not as easy to strive for it. If it were easy, there would be a lot more successful people in this world.

So how do you work on achieving a goal? What can you do in order to fulfill your dreams? In this chapter, you will learn how to create long-term goals, formulate steps on how to achieve them, and visualize the end result that serves as the beacon for your journey.

Aristotle emphasizes the importance of goal-setting by citing three steps. Over two thousand years ago, he said the first step is to "have a definite, clear, practical idea." This is your goal or your objective. The next step in Aristotle's quote is to gather all the necessary means to achieve the identified goals. These means should be adjusted if necessary so that they are targeted towards that end. These means include "wisdom, money, materials, and methods."

Create Your Goals

The human mind is a complex organ capable of so many great things, including the ability to create. Your dreams are your personal creations, and they are limitlessness. Dreams enable you to freely explore all possibilities in detail without the constraints of the physical world. Through your dreams, you can tap into your desires and realize your true goals in life.

To create your long-term life goals, you first have to free your mind from the limitations of logic and structure that are all too familiar in the physical world. Simply allow your creativity to flow. Allow yourself to dream and connect with your heart's desire. Do not even attempt to analyze anything and simply let your mind wander. Minimize any external influences that might affect your mind from creating your true life goals. Forget about the pressure to please others, to fit into a mold shaped by society, and to follow the path that everyone else is following.

When you really think about it, successful goal-setting is driven by motivation, and you can only be truly motivated if you have a genuine desire for something. When you are positively motivated, you will no longer feel stressed as you pursue your goals. True goals give you a strong sense of purpose, while goals set for you by others will only make you feel burdened. Working toward something you do not really desire will feel too laborious for you and might lead to frustration and regret.

To create your goals, take right now as an opportunity to delve deep into your mind and think of a dream you have always wanted to fulfill. It should be something that will make you feel satisfied with your life once you have achieved it. If you are having trouble with what this is, try these two simple exercises:

- **Exercise 1:** Get a piece of paper and a pen. Start listing down the following items: Financial Status, Personal Growth, Physical Well-being, Emotional Balance, Career, Academics, Relationships, Social Life, and Spirituality. You can add more items if you feel like it.

  Once you have completed your list, rate your degree of satisfaction in each of these aspects of your life using a scale of 1 to 10 with 10 as the highest.

  As you rate these aspects of your life, you will be forced to assess your level of satisfaction in as far as each aspect is concerned. When you are done, you will have a good sense of which aspects of your life you would want to improve. You can make use of this information to create your goals.

- **Exercise 2:** In this exercise, you will pretend that you are in the final moments of your life. Find a place where you can be quiet and where you will not be disturbed for a couple of minutes. In your chosen room, the first thing to do is to lie down on your back. Close your eyes and be completely still.

  Now, imagine yourself lying in bed about to die. As morbid as this seems, the next step is actually life-changing for many people: reflect on the dreams that you have always had and never got around to chasing. Consider whether you regret not having achieved any of them. Among your dreams, highlight the ones that make you feel the most regretful. These dreams are your life goals.

Regardless of if your goals are large or small, the important thing is that the thought of achieving them makes you feel elated. Ask yourself, "What do I want?" Do this aloud. State the question clearly and answer it out loud too. Be clear in stating what exactly it is that you want. Dwell on this mental image.

Then, close your eyes and come up with a vivid mental image of what your goal is. As you imagine it, notice how you feel. Do you get that "warm and fuzzy" feeling all over? Do you feel stronger and more energetic or calm and at peace? Does your heart beat faster? These are symptoms of desire.

Now that you have your goals, quickly write them down and hold onto them. In the next chapter, you will learn how to formulate a practical sequence of steps that will guide you throughout your journey to achieving each of your goals.

Chapter 2 - Formulate A Plan

The one thing that can turn a dream into a goal is a plan. Once you have a long-term goal you are determined to achieve, you will need to come up with specific steps on how to achieve it. Think of each step as short-term goals that will ultimately lead you to achieving the long-term one. These short-term goals can be further broken down into daily and weekly tasks that you need to accomplish.

The easiest way to create these steps is to find a quiet spot where you can think clearly without being disturbed. After all, planning does require a lot of focus. Have a pen and paper ready to map out the steps you need to take to reach your goal.

Goal Statement. If you do not know where to begin, start by writing down your goal in the form of a single statement. The best way to word this statement is to use positive action words that inspire you to push through with your plan every time you read it, even when the going gets tough. It should also remain relevant to you even after a few years, especially while you are still in the middle of working toward the goal. You must also make sure the statement is specific. For instance, if your goal is to lose weight, your goal statement should not just say, "Lose weight!" Make it more specific like: "Burn 20 pounds and maintain my ideal healthy weight of 125 pounds!" Of course, you should make sure that 125 pounds is indeed the recommended body weight for your body type. Your goal should be to become fit and to stay within a healthy weight range.

Lastly, right next to your goal statement, you should set a date within which you intend to accomplish your specific goal. This date should be realistic. This date is temporary in the sense that you can adjust it later on once you have formulated the actual steps.

For example, if you are about to graduate from high school and your goal is to earn a degree in Accountancy and pass the necessary exams before you turn 25, a good goal statement would be: "to study accountancy and take the Board Exam in the year ____."

Goal Outline. After the goal statement comes the challenging part, which is to brainstorm on the necessary steps you need to take. You can break down large steps into smaller, more manageable pieces as well, so you will not feel overwhelmed by what needs to be done. You can do plenty of research on what you can do first in order to attain your goal. Once you have collected all of the necessary steps, you can now organize them into a single outline. It would be even better to state a deadline next to each task in order to avoid procrastination.

For example, if you have just obtained a Bachelor's degree and your goal is to become a lawyer, the first major step is to find a good law school. Underneath that major step, create a list of tasks that you need to accomplish, such as getting an application form, studying the admission tips, and preparing for the Law School Admissions Test.

In outline form, your goal would then look something like this:

Goal Statement: "To become a Lawyer at the age of 27"

I. Find a Law School by April 25.

    A. Get an application form from (university) by April 15.

    B. Study the admission tips from (university) law school website/forms by April 18.

    C. Prepare for LSAT between April and June.

        a) Purchase sample tests to practice on before April 15.

        b) Obtain the list of requirements for LSAT before May 10.

As you can see, the outline will really help you out in determining exactly what you need to do, starting with your major goal and the mini-goals and moving right down to the daily tasks that are crucial to your success. You can always add or change some details to your outline as you go along. It is also good to know that an outline can only be as detailed as you would want it to be. You can also choose not to specify the tasks under each mini-goal in the outline itself. Instead, you can use the outline as a guide for composing the daily to-do list that is in line with your goals.

Once you have your outline, the next step is to put all the steps into a layout.

Layout. While the outline serves as a general guide to reaching your goal, the layout serves as your "blueprint." Layouts are easier to look at compared to a detailed outline, and they look more inspiring, too.

Having a clear and organized layout is a great way to map out your goal. It gives you a bird's eye view from where you are now to where you want to be in each step of the way toward your destination.

There are several layouts you can choose from to turn your steps into a systematic flow toward your goal. The ones that will be discussed in detail here are the Flowchart, the Timeline, and the Checklist.

- **The Flowchart.** The easiest way to look at how your plan will progress is by designing a flowchart that will show each step toward your goal. A flow chart not only summarizes the steps that you need to take, but also creates a more "fluid" mental image of what you need to do as opposed to an outline. The best part about a flowchart is that you can decorate it however you like, and post it in a spot where you can see it every day.

- **The Timeline.** If you have at least two goals you want to work on simultaneously, then you will want to create a timeline. This will help you coordinate varying tasks and steps for multiple goals within a single layout without feeling overwhelmed. It is recommended that you create a horizontal timeline instead of a vertical one because it is easier to organize different goals in this way.

- **The Checklist.** A checklist is every organized person's go-to tool. There is a certain sense of satisfaction in ticking the box next to each accomplished task. Checklists are so versatile since you can use them for both major and minor goals. You can even make your outline more interactive by turning it into a checklist instead.

Clearly, layouts also serve as tools that will help you stick to the plan and keep track of your progress. You can even use all three of them to help you out.

For instance, after creating your outline, you can design a nifty looking flowchart and post it in front of your work desk to serve as a daily reminder of your goals. For multiple goals, you can design a timeline that will also serve as a tracker for the deadlines to your mini-goals. Finally, you can use the checklist on a regular basis to help you manage the tasks under each mini-goal.

Once you have a plan, your goal will start to look a lot more achievable. The more detailed your plan is and the more specific your deadlines are, the more successful you will likely be. Just remember to be flexible and adapt to any changes that need to be made in your plans.

Visualize the Finish Line

Now that you have a specific major goal and a detailed plan, a very important step that follows is to visualize the completion of your goal. A lot of people fail to do this step, which is why so many great plans simply go to waste.

Visualization works because it enables you to "see" in your mind the outcome that you desire, which helps keep you motivated and confident in achieving your goal. Even professional athletes engage in visualization in preparation for a major sports event. Research has proven that when athletes visualize, they become more focused, coordinated, and driven. Furthermore, visualization helps reduce feelings of fear, impatience, and negative pressures.

When you visualize your goal, your brain remembers the details more vividly as compared to simply looking at a list of words and numbers that represent your goals. The mental image in your visualization triggers an impulse in the brain that signals the neurons to act it out. In other words, visualization leads to actual performance.

There are two kinds of visualization. The one wherein you visualize the completion of your goal is called "outcome visualization." The second is called "process visualization," and it involves you visualizing every action you need to take in order to get closer to your goal. Using both kinds of visualization will strengthen your dedication to your goal.

To explain in detail how you can use visualization to your advantage, take a look at the following example:

Let's say your main goal is to lose 10 pounds in 3 months. You have developed a plan to exercise for 30 minutes every day, avoid sugar and carbohydrates in all your meals, and eat more lean protein, fruits and vegetables.

To use the outcome visualization, close your eyes and envision yourself ten years ago when you still weighed 10 pounds less. You immerse yourself in the visualization and actually feel yourself having more energy and confidence. You are able to wear the clothes you have always wanted, and you get to do amazing athletic stuff, like rock climbing, deep sea diving, and distance running. You feel inspired by the mental image, and you do not want to lose any time in working toward it as efficiently as you can.

Now, the first step you need to take toward your goal is to get rid of all the sugary and high carbohydrate foods in your home. You find this to be a difficult task, because you are attached to your well-stocked pantry. However, with the help of process visualization you can conquer those obstacles. Close your eyes and visualize yourself going to your kitchen and getting an empty cardboard box labeled "donations." In your visualization, your mind actually came up with the idea to donate the food to the poor. You fill the box with the food items you have banned from your diet, and you seal the box shut. Then, you drive off to donate it. As you visualized, you realize that it is not such a hard thing to do. In fact, your mind tells you that it is quite achievable. After your visualization, you allow the mental image to guide you through the first step toward your goal.

Congratulations on finally having a specific goal, coming up with a detailed plan, and embracing the principles of visualization. However, this is just the start of your exciting journey toward fulfilling your dreams. There are still other aspects, such as hard work, practice, and perfect timing that need to be done. Anyway, the challenge of reaching for your goals is a huge part of what makes life interesting.

That is why, in the next chapter, you will learn how to make adjustments within yourself and in your surroundings, so your plan will be a success.

Chapter 3 - Make Adjustments

How you reach your goals depends highly upon your attitude and abilities. By becoming aware of your inner resources, you will be able to maximize them and accomplish the tasks in line with your goals.

In this chapter, you will get to know yourself a little more and find out how you can develop a healthy self-esteem, positive outlook, and strong determination – the three key factors that will help you become successful.

Invest in Knowledge, Skills and Experience

School is not the only place from which you can obtain knowledge. Life's experiences have taught people so many things beyond the textbooks and teachers' lectures. However, it is an important step to compare your current knowledge with your plans because it is possible that you may still need to gain more knowledge before you can move on to the next step.

For example, if your goal is to get promoted from trainer to training manager, you must first know the criteria for the position. Another example is when you make plans to run your own small business. You will need to gain knowledge first on how to run a small business efficiently and legally before you can make plans to turn it into a success.

Gaining knowledge and experience does not only require learning, but it also entails unlearning and relearning. There are old habits that need to be replaced, especially if you are following methodology that is consistently being updated. It is highly recommended that you constantly develop your skills and aim to acquire new sets of skills as you go along. You need to especially take note of the skills that are required for you to achieve your goals.

Since your goals depend a lot on your knowledge, skills and experience, here are the steps you can follow to maximize and improve your abilities to boost your chances of success, using the goal of becoming an ESL teacher in a foreign country as an example:

- **Clearly state the knowledge and skills that your main goal requires.** Create a checklist of the books you need to read, courses you need to take, and certifications you need to obtain. Organize these skills in a linear, chronological order and note which items are prerequisites to other items. If there are specific dates for applying to and taking certain courses and tests, make sure to note them next to the appropriate item on your checklist.

  Example: Since you want to work as an ESL teacher in a foreign country, you will need to gather the list of requirements that will qualify you for the position. This will include obtaining teaching and ESL certifications. In order to gain these, you will then need to check the knowledge and skills required for that. Compare these requirements with your own existing knowledge and skills.

  Take mock tests to assess your existing knowledge and set of skills. It is important to take a self-assessment before you take the actual exam. This will allow you to prepare mentally, physically, and emotionally. After all, you will not know the areas you are good at or the areas that need improvement unless you test yourself first.

Example: Before taking the tests that will determine whether you qualify as an ESL teacher or not, it is best to practice with review booklets and possibly even take review classes for the assessments. Allot a specific number of hours every day to prepare for the tests, so you can establish the right habits that will help you get passing marks.

- **Gain work experience that is relevant to your goal.** Once you have obtained the knowledge and skills, the next step is to continue honing them by gaining experience. Apply for jobs that enable you to exercise the knowledge and skills you have obtained.

Example: Since your goal is to travel the world as an ESL teacher, you will need to gain as much experience as possible in teaching English to non-native speakers. Sign up as a full-time or part-time teacher at a local or online language institute that will provide you with a certificate of employment later on. You can also volunteer to teach non-native speakers in educational outreach programs.

- **Build a network.** As you continue to build upon the knowledge, skills, and experience that bring you closer to your goals, this will also be a great opportunity for you to make friends and establish connections with the people from the same industry. Learn how to socialize and maintain relationships with the people you meet. The more people you are well-acquainted with, the more opportunities will come your way.

Example: Since your plan is to work in a foreign country, you will definitely need contacts from the country you want to work in. You will not meet these people overnight, so start building connections while you are still gaining experience. Make friends within your workplace and learn as much as you can about how you can reach out to the language institutes in the other country through the people you meet.

Clearly, it takes time, effort and lots of practice to get to a specific goal. However, it takes more than just knowledge, skills and experience to chase your dreams. Your attitude plays a central role behind all of these factors.

Have a Positive Attitude

The good news is that you can actually change your attitude if you have the will to do so. A positive, can-do attitude is what will propel you toward your main goal. It goes without saying that an attitude adjustment is definitely worth the time, effort, and energy. In fact, the right attitude makes all the difference, because it is the driving force behind everything you do and all the choices you make.

If you feel the need to adjust your attitude in favor of your main goal, you can start by developing the three key areas, namely: your outlook on life, your willingness to learn, and your self-esteem. To improve all of these qualities, you can start by adapting a simple daily routine that will enable you to do some self-reflection:

Develop a positive outlook on life. The world is not always full of happiness, but that does not mean you should sulk when the rain starts to pour. Having a positive outlook is necessary for problem solving because your mind becomes good at seeking solutions instead of dwelling on the negativity.

To gain a positive outlook, you can start the day by planning at least three positive experiences you want to accomplish before the day ends. Then, before going to bed, reflect on the positive experiences you have had, including the ones you actually did not plan to do. Doing this enables you to add more value to each waking day.

Another habit you can adopt for a positive outlook is to counteract negative thoughts that enter your mind. For instance, if a little voice inside your head suddenly whispers, "You don't have the skills for that!" you counter it by asking yourself, "Will that thought help me toward my goal?" Let the negative thought fade away, and let your mind focus on how to solve the problem in front of you instead.

Cultivate your willingness to learn. Once you stop learning, you stop growing. Indeed, as long as you continue to exercise your mind, it will never stop absorbing. Be open to learning and discovering new things about yourself and in your surroundings. If you stumble across something that seems completely alien to you, let it inspire you to be more curious. There might be times when certain principles you have been following all your life are challenged. Try to see things from the other perspective. You might find something you have been missing all this time.

If you do not know something, it is perfectly alright. Go ahead and ask questions and then research about your newly found information. As you make mistakes while you learn, acknowledge them and see them as a way for you to constantly improve. Do not become the person who lives a stagnant life because he refuses to own up to his mistakes.

Boost your self-esteem. Your own opinion of yourself is what constitutes your self-esteem. It is important to be your own best cheerleader, especially when it comes to satisfying your life goals. No one else lives your life except you, so do not depend on others to make you feel good about yourself.

If you have been suffering from low self-esteem, now is the time to give yourself more credit for all your accomplishments in life, whether they are big or small. Take the time to recall your past successes and feel proud of how far you have come.

You can also come up with positive affirmations that will help you feel more confident in your abilities. Put these affirmations on paper and take them with you whenever you can. You can also look for a motivational quote that will remind you to work on boosting your self-esteem. Set it as the wallpaper on your computer and mobile phone, or print it and post it in front of your desk.

Learn to take care of yourself, as well, because what you see on the outside makes a difference on how you feel on the inside. Learn how to dress well, spoil yourself with a spa treatment (even if it is just a foot soak at home), and take better care of your health.

Lastly, avoid comparing yourself to other people. This can be a particularly difficult thing to do, especially in light of social media trends these days. Just remember that the things people post online are only the highlights of their lives; it is normal to avoid posting about the less stellar side. Whenever you see someone achieving something great, learn to feel genuinely happy for them. Use their success as an inspiration for yourself.   If they can do it, you definitely can, too!

Prioritize Good Health and Energy

Your health and energy levels have a huge impact on your ability to work towards your goals. Low energy naturally leads to low quality output, and health issues will certainly hinder the accomplishment of tasks and offset your self-imposed deadlines. This is why it is important to make adjustments to your lifestyle, so you can boost your energy levels and improve your performance.

Take a step back from your everyday routine and assess how you have been treating your body and mind lately. Try answering the following questions to help you reflect on your health:

- Do you get adequate sleep?

- Do you engage in regular exercise (for instance, at least three times a week)?

- Do you eat more fruits and vegetables than fast foods?

- Do you monitor your alcohol intake?

- Do you always rely on coffee or an energy drink just to get through the day?

- Do you minimize your consumption of sugar and simple carbohydrates?

If you have been feeling unwell recently or suffering from fluctuating energy levels, it would be a good idea to read health and fitness books. Better yet, consult a physician or a dietitian in order to make the necessary changes to your lifestyle.

Having a long-term goal means you need to have a long lifespan as well. There is no point in pushing yourself too hard to attain your goals if your own body is suffering in the process. Here are some simple tips on how to keep your energy level high to sustain you through each day and enable you to accomplish your goal-centered tasks:

- Listen to what your body tells you. People have different natural work and rest cycles, which is why some people can work nonstop for hours without feeling tired but others need more frequent breaks.

  For a week, monitor how long you can work until you honestly feel like resting. You should also record the times within the day when you feel most productive, and schedule your most important tasks during those periods.

- Make exercise a priority. A lot of people always use the excuse of "not having enough time" for exercise. It is actually a lot like saying, "I don't have enough time to be healthy." Even light to moderate exercise is enough to boost your endurance, a necessity when it comes to maintaining high energy levels.

Set an appointment with yourself to exercise for at least 20 minutes every day or 40 minutes every other day. Choose an exercise which you are genuinely fond of. There are plenty of choices out there, such as running, swimming, badminton, dancing, and so on. Invest in exercising, such as buying a high quality pair of shoes or signing up for gym membership. Your health is your most precious investment.

- Surround yourself with healthy food. Likewise, stay away from unhealthy choices. If eating healthy diet is not one of your major goals yet, it should be. What you feed your body has an instant effect on your energy, so if you have been feeling bloated and tired lately, then you seriously need to reconsider your daily food choices.

  Get rid of all the unhealthy choices at home and build a grocery list full of nutritious foods you will actually eat on a regular basis. If you do not know how to prepare healthy food, then pick up a healthy diet cookbook that will show you how. It is also a good idea to set specific limitations to eating unhealthy foods. For example, decide to not have a slice of cake for 30 days after you have eaten one. Lastly and most importantly, learn to love eating healthy foods. Your preference for certain foods is all a state of mind.

- Minimize your caffeine intake. While caffeine does work its magic on boosting your energy levels instantly, it still has detrimental, long-term effects. For instance, you will become dependent on it. It will also keep you from going to bed on time and getting adequate sleep.

On days when you have particularly low energy levels, choose to drink green tea in the morning instead of coffee. Green tea also contains caffeine, but not in such high amounts as coffee. It also has antioxidants that serve to cleanse the body. Avoid drinking coffee after lunch time, otherwise you will find it difficult to lie still, fall asleep, and recharge for the next day.

Chapter 4 - Conquer Your Fears

No matter how knowledgeable, skilled, and experienced you are, and no matter how physically fit you may be, you can still become vulnerable to the roadblock called fear, which is often present on the road to your goals. The good news is that you can overcome your fears by becoming aware of them and learning how to maintain a positive attitude through it all.

Fear is a natural feeling that occurs when one starts to imagine negative possibilities that might take place in the future. It is easy to think negatively, because the future is always uncertain. Fear starts with the negative thought in the form of a question, "What if I fail?" and then it starts to play with your emotions, making you feel restless and nervous. The truth about fear is that it is irrational. How can one be fearful of something that has not happened yet? While fear is initially meant to protect you, it mainly causes unnecessary stress and self-destruction. Fear may even be the only thing keeping you from living life to the fullest. It even turns the things we used to enjoy into a chore.

To beat fear and push through with your long-term goals, it is important to have faith in your plan. Yes, there will be times when things do not go exactly as you want them to, but you can always come up with an even better alternative along the way.

Here is a short guide on how you can conquer your fears as you continue to work toward your goal:

Break down a Goliath. If your problem seems too big to handle, you can actually take a step back from the emotional turmoil and pretend you are your own personal assistant. Your job is to break down the huge problem into smaller, more doable tasks. Suddenly, your big problem will not look so overbearing anymore. For instance, if you are worried that your goal to start a restaurant might fail, then why not choose to do made-to-order catering services first? It does not mean you are downgrading; all it means is that you are setting realistic expectations based on your risk appetite.

Take a leap of faith. Perfectionists usually suffer the most when it comes to fear, especially if they do not want to "tarnish a perfect record." Unfortunately, being too much of a perfectionist will hold you back from the real opportunities. Many successful entrepreneurs started out with an idea and a prayer. They took a leap of faith to see if it will work out, and sometimes it does. Just remember when it all comes down to your big goal, your biggest asset is being alive. It is better to have faith in what you are planning to achieve and then go for it, rather than beat yourself up over the "what if's" for the remainder of your days.

Openly acknowledge your fears. In order to beat your fears, you must know exactly what they are, so you can come up with ways to overcome them. Whenever fear strikes you, get a pen and paper and let your thoughts flow freely. Later on in the day, read what you have written and then figure out what the source of this fear is. Decide whether you can do something about it or if you should accept it as a part of the process.

Accept and let go. When something just does not work out the way you want it to, there really is no point in dwelling on it. Past experiences might have bruised you, but never let them destroy your present moment and the possibility of success in the future. Continue to work toward your goal, and simply make adjustments to plans that no longer fit into the equation. You will just have to accept and let go of the things you cannot change and work with what you have now.

As you continue to plan and accomplish each task that brings you closer to the fulfillment of your dreams, you are also growing as a person. Practice being flexible and you can adapt to just about any hurdle that comes your way. Be determined to reach for your goals, and "keep your eyes on the prize."

Chapter 5 - Form Winning Habits

Everyday life is made up of a system of habits. These habits can add up over time, leading you to the lifestyle you are currently living. Your major goals are affected immensely by your habits, which is why you need to make changes right this very moment if your habits are negatively affecting your plans. Even Warren Buffet, one of the richest men in the world, once said, "Chains of habit are too light to be felt until they are too heavy to be broken."

According to psychologists, a habit is an automatic pattern of behavior that is in reaction to a particular situation. A habit is also usually acquired through frequent repetition. How you wake up in the morning and get ready for the day is already a set of habits. How you think whenever you face an unexpected circumstance is also a habit. To accomplish your goals, you must establish the habits that will lead you to them.

Habitual Thought Patterns

Observable behavior or actions are not the only ones that constitute habits. How you think actually plays a central role in everything you do. To put it simply, how you think affects how you feel and how you feel affects how you behave. Ultimately, how you behave leads to the results that you have in your hands now.

A habitual thought pattern is like a reflex wherein your mind comes up with either a positive or negative thought as it reacts to an experience. If you take some time to reflect on how you would normally react to a situation, can you say your habitual thought pattern is more positive than negative? For example, if your major goal is to get married and you have already started making plans when you found out that your significant other cheated on you, how would you respond to that scenario?

Most people's initial response would naturally be to freak out and get mad or depressed. However, a person with healthy habitual thought patterns would then be able to get up, brush it off, and devise a way out of this mess. On the other hand, the person who has unhealthy habitual thought patterns would continue to wallow in his or her misery and probably even do things that will put him in a much worse position than before.

So what can you do to improve your habitual thought patterns? In the previous chapter, you learned about how to counteract negative thoughts, and this is a great method to practice.

Another method that you can apply is called the Alexander technique, created by Frederick Matthias Alexander. It involves stopping unnecessary mental stress in everyday routines. Based on the Alexander technique, experts nowadays advise avoiding starting your thought processes with phrases such as "I will try to...," "I can't do...," "I am not allowed to...," "I have to...," "I only like...," "I don't like...," and "I am too afraid/shy/unqualified..." These thoughts imply limitations, lack of motivation, and lack of flexibility. Furthermore, these habitual thought patterns unconsciously cause you to put a label on yourself, such as not being good enough for something or someone. Instead, according to the Alexander technique, you can exercise your free will by choosing to think differently from here on out. Whenever a self-defeating thought crosses your mind, follow up with a thought that starts with, "I am free to be...," "I have the freedom to...," "I always have a choice...," and "I have the ability to..." You will soon realize that, by embracing your freedom to choose, you can achieve your goals more efficiently.

Habitual Language

How you communicate, whether it is with yourself or with others, affects you and your performance just as much as your habitual thoughts do. The words you choose to express yourself say a lot about you, and it will also direct you down a particular path. For example, if you are working on a problem and you suddenly blurt out, "This is difficult. I can't do this!" your attitude will certainly be affected by what your words and then you will indeed find the task difficult. But if you say, "There must be a solution to this, I know it!" your mind will find ways to fulfill this statement.

The main difference between thought patterns and actual words is that the latter has a bigger impact on your actions. For instance, there is a difference between thinking, "I can't do this!" and actually saying it out loud. Therefore, as you continue to work on improving your habitual thought patterns, you must also avoid saying negative words out loud.

One important habit you can start learning is to change negative statements into inquisitive questions. For example, if your mind churns out the thought, "If I do finish this..." you can counteract it by saying out loud, "When can I finish this?" If your start to think, "I'll try to learn this...," you should say, "How can I learn this effectively?" and if you start to think, "This does not seem useful..." you say, "How would this be useful?"

As you can see, you should never underestimate the strength of your words. From here on out, practice filtering your choice of words – the ones in your mind and the ones you speak. Of course, it is perfectly alright to have the occasional slip of the tongue, such as calling yourself "silly." Just remember to consciously counteract your self-defeating thoughts and words, and you will surely gain the confidence to face your challenges.

Social Habits

An important factor that most people overlook when it comes to working toward their goals is the people they spend most of their time with. As you know, human beings are social creatures, which means your social connections have great impact on your plans.

You must know every person in your life that can help you reach your goals. To do this, you can make a list of these people, starting with your immediate family and close friends, who can also be your support group. You should also include your co-workers and employer, as well as your subordinates, if any. Clients and acquaintances should be included too.

Once you have your list, aim to build strong and healthy relationships with these people. On the other hand, if there are individuals in your list who, unfortunately, are more destructive than helpful, consider spending less time with them.

It would also be a good idea to practice your social skills, especially if these are in line with your goals. It never hurts to be kind and supportive of others and to engage in meaningful conversations with them. Many successful people do not even separate their professional relationships from their personal ones; everything just boils down to the word "relationships." They treat their clients as warmly as they would treat their friends, all limitations and formalities considered.

Of course, improving your social habits does not necessarily mean letting go of who you are. Simply take into consideration the fact that people do change for the better, and that includes you. Whether you are an introvert or an extrovert, there are always means for you to socialize and network with other people. If you feel like you need to know more people, do not be shy to join organizations that share your interests.

Chapter 6 - Harness Time And Make Effort

In this chapter, you will learn the most valuable skills to help you establish a goal-centered everyday routine. Specifically, you will learn how to improve your time management skills, set priorities, and train yourself to become more disciplined. Without these skills, it will be difficult, if not altogether impossible, to attain your ultimate goals in life.

Self-Discipline

The biggest enemy you will face throughout your journey toward your goals is called an "excuse." Excuse comes in a multitude of forms: someone had a bad childhood, does not have enough time, or does not have enough money. Any other rationalization or justification for failing to take action in their lives is an excuse.

The one thing that a person needs to overcome all of his excuses is by imposing self-discipline. This is not a new concept. Philosophers and successful individuals throughout the centuries have been talking about how important self-discipline is. Without it, there is no chance of fulfilling your goals.

To set realistic expectations, you must know that gaining self-discipline is not a walk in the park. It requires a lot of time and effort to harness, and it is something a person should consistently practice throughout his or her entire life. The average person can achieve far greater things when he or she has self-discipline.

Going back to the enemy called excuse, you must know that there are two main driving forces behind it, and they are aptly called "easy way out" and "instant gratification." The worst part is that they both go hand in hand.

Whenever a person is taking the easy way out, he or she wants to do things the easy way, even if this is not the right way. People who fall for get rich quick schemes or buy products that deliver ridiculously impossible "instant" results are those who have listened to the "easy way out" excuse. By constantly seeking faster ways to do something, usually halfheartedly so as to get things over with, you develop the bad habit of not putting in real effort that will actually reel in true success.

Instant gratification is an even worse enemy of self-discipline, because it equips itself with powerful weapons in the form of temptations. Instant gratification means deciding to do something fun and easy right now, rather than choosing to do what is right, simply because fun and easy make you feel good. You succumb to instant gratification each time you choose not to pay off your debt or put money into your emergency fund, and instead go on a shopping spree. You also do that whenever you decide to eat junk food and not exercise when you are supposed to. The sad part is that the more often you choose to instantly gratify yourself, the harder it will be for you to conquer this habit.

If you want to become self-disciplined, you must be prepared to make changes in your life. This includes making hard choices, such as taking control over your emotions and appetites. You would even have to deny yourself quite a number of pleasures.

Of course, you are definitely not exercising self-discipline just for the heck of it. People become self-disciplined because they are investing in themselves for the long-term. That is to say, they are putting off satisfaction now, so they can fulfill their goals and enjoy much bigger rewards in the long run. After all, time has proven that the most successful individuals think in the long-term.

Each time you are proactively exercising self-discipline, you are actually looking into the future (more specifically, your goals), and then you connect it with the present moment. You do this for the reason that your future depends on what you are doing now.

To become a self-disciplined person, you will need to practice it regularly. It will be hard at first, but as you continue to do it, it gets a whole lot easier until it becomes a part of your routine. The most amazing part is that once you have developed self-discipline, all the other good habits will follow.

The first step to become self-disciplined is to strongly commit to a particular behavior. Right now, choose a single behavior you want to stick to, such as getting up early in the morning or studying for at least two hours a day. After you have chosen the behavior, the next step is to make a firm decision to never make any exceptions and excuses.

Every time you fail to stick to the commitment, and there is a chance that you will, you must resolve to just pick yourself up and continue to practice self-discipline until the behavior becomes more natural to you.

Once you have established self-discipline in one behavior, you can move on to another one. You can always choose more than one type of behavior, but then again you must go back to the basic principle of divide and conquer. Some people find it easier to introduce self-discipline into their routine by taking it one habit at a time. If you are confident in your ability to change, however, you can go right ahead take more aggressive steps in tackling your undesirable habits.

Schedule

Keeping a regularly updated schedule is an essential part of goal-setting. A schedule serves as a detailed guide of what you need to do next, and when exactly you need to do it. A dream cannot be a goal without a deadline, and a deadline can only be set when there is a schedule.

In fact, following a schedule optimizes your time and efficiency. For instance, it compels you to complete a specific task before a set time. Remember that if you do not adhere to the deadline, you will offset all the other tasks you have already planned. With a schedule, you will no longer waste any time wondering what you should do next because you have already set a specific time and date for important tasks.

There are plenty of schedule formats you can choose from, but the most recommended one is called time blocking. A lot of successful individuals swear by the effectiveness of time blocking, and you can make use of it, too. Time blocking is when you dedicate a set amount of minutes or hours to a specific task without succumbing to distractions. It works by being simple and strengthening your focus.

To use time blocking to create your daily schedule, follow these steps:

Prepare a layout that you can use for time blocking. You can use an organizer with a pen or paper, or you can use a digital device, preferably with a spreadsheet interface. The suggested way for setting time blocks is by assigning the first column for the actual time blocks (say, 15 minutes per time block). The second column will contain the description for the specific task that you need to focus on per time block. Lastly, the third column serves as a "notes" section where you can jot down pertinent information regarding the set task for each time block.

You can color-code your time blocks based on their level of importance and specific purpose. For instance, the color red would mean "urgent," the color blue could be "personal time" such as your break time or for bathing, the color purple could be for "work" time, such as the time you spend at the office, and the gold ones can be the tasks that are in line with your goals, in other words, your priorities.

Start with your biggest priority. Identify the most important task you need to do for the day. Naturally, this important task should be in relation to your main goal. It is recommended that you allot the first two to four hours of your day to working on your goal-related tasks. For example, if your goal for this year is to pass the comprehensive exam in graduate school, then the first thing you need to do upon waking up is to dedicate two to three hours to studying.

Think of it this way: if you have not tackled the most important task for the day yet, all other tasks simply serve as distractions.

Follow the fifteen-minute time block principle. According to many time management experts, fifteen minutes is a long enough period of time for someone to spend on a particular task. Of course, longer tasks require multiple fifteen minute time blocks, but time spent on leisure or rest such as your break time should not exceed fifteen minutes. The rule of thumb is for an average person to take one quick (fifteen minute) break in between two hours of productive work. You might be able to do more than two hours, or less than fifteen minutes for break time. If you do, simply make adjustments that suit you best.

Here is an example of how to use the fifteen-minute time block principle: Let's say your number one priority is to study for a major exam, and you have decided to schedule that in the morning because you know that you can concentrate well during that time. You can probably allot four fifteen-minute time blocks (equivalent to an hour) for studying without stopping not even to check your phone or email. You can set a timer to remind you that your time block is up. Then, you can set one fifteen-minute time block to take a break. During this time, you can go ahead and surf the internet, reply to personal emails, and scroll through your Facebook feeds. After that, you can set another four fifteen minutes for some more studying.

Block time for making plans. Naturally, you should also dedicate a time block for making plans and preparing for the next day. This time will also provide you with an excellent opportunity for reflecting on where you are now and what else you need to do in order to get closer to your goals.

What many successful and organized people usually do is allot an entire day per year for planning out their whole year, an hour every month for making plans for the whole month, and an hour within the week to create weekly plans. For daily planning and reflection, they usually set aside fifteen minutes of their day as well.

Block time for rest and relaxation. Aside from focusing simply on productivity and working toward your goals, you must also set time blocks for vacations and weekends for yourself and your family. After all, there is no point in living a life full of plans and goals when you do not even have the time to enjoy yourself.

Upon using time blocks, you will learn that time blocking is a great way to let you know where your plans are taking you and what you want to get done. Just remember to set your daily schedule the night before. That way, you will be able to wake up refreshed and ready, and the morning will only be left for reviewing the schedule that you have already set and for getting started immediately on your tasks.

Priorities

Making plans alone is not a guarantee that you will be successful. A lot can happen in a year, a week, or even a day that will prevent you from working toward your goals. The main reason why so many plans fail to push through is that the goal setters were not able to distinguish between what is urgent and what is important.

Urgent tasks are the ones that demand your attention immediately, such as your work, your chores, and keeping up with the bills you need to pay before the end of the month. These are the things you spend most of your hours on regularly. Important tasks, on the other hand, are the ones that are in line with your goals. They are also the ones that people normally neglect even though these very tasks are essential to their health, such as exercise. The sad thing is that people will always have too many urgent tasks that they need to do, unless they do something about it.

Fortunately, there is a way for you to set your priorities straight and make time for the truly important things in your life. Here is how you can do it:

Write down the tasks you usually do every day. These would include preparing and eating your meals, commuting to and from work, working at the office, and surfing the internet. Be as specific as you can, so that you would know exactly what is eating up most of your time.

Add the tasks that are in line with your main goals. Using the same list of everyday tasks, include all the things that you need to do to get closer to your goal. For instance, if your goal is to lose weight, you can add exercise and grocery shopping for healthy foods in the list.

Separate the tasks into "urgent" and "important." Divide a separate piece of paper into two, then label the first column as "urgent" and the second as "important." With the list of tasks you have just made, decide on the column under which to put each task. It would be even better if you enumerate the tasks based on their level of urgency and importance. That way you can find out which tasks are essential to your daily routine.

Whittle the list of urgent tasks. You will need to let go of some urgent yet unimportant tasks, so you can make room for the more important ones. For instance, you can set aside a fifteen minutes of your day at most to check your emails and social networking sites. You can also delegate some of your urgent tasks to someone else, such as an assistant. You can even resort to a few "life hacks" such as how to prepare a week's worth of meals within a single day, or how to cut down on your time for doing the laundry and other such tasks.

Try out your new routine. Now that you have sorted out your priorities, you can move on to creating a new schedule for yourself set for an entire week. See if it all fits perfectly according to your goal-centered plans. After the week ends, check to see if any adjustments need to be made. Check if there is a need to delegate more urgent tasks to others or to remove certain tasks from your list altogether. It is all a matter of trial and error until you can finally get into a new system of habits that will take you closer to your goal.

Always remember that every single thing you repeatedly do becomes a habit. And once habits are developed, they are pretty difficult to break. By creating a routine filled with productive habits and by applying self-discipline to stick to it, you can achieve all of your goals. Once you have fulfilled those goals, you can always look back at all the sacrifices you made and the hard work you put in, and then tell yourself it was all worth it.

Conclusion

I hope this book was able to help you to realize that you need to take more aggressive steps to succeed in achieving your goals. It is not impossible. All you need to do is take action in the right direction and with the right attitude.

The next step is to start defining your goals in more specific terms and making a plan to get you there sooner rather than later. Take stock of the "tools" you have and continue equipping yourself with the right mindset, knowledge, and habits for success. Continue practicing self-discipline and forming good habits that will enable you to be at your best every day. Let this be the start of a better and happier lifestyle for you.

Thank you and good luck!

www.ingramcontent.com/pod-product-compliance
Lightning Source LLC
Chambersburg PA
CBHW070717180526
45167CB00004B/1513